DISCOVERING SACRED TEXTS

Series editor:
W. Owen Cole

The Torah

Douglas Charing

HEINEMANN

Heinemann Educational
a division of Heinemann Publishers (Oxford) Ltd
Halley Court, Jordan Hill, Oxford OX2 8EJ

OXFORD LONDON EDINBURGH
MADRID ATHENS BOLOGNA PARIS
MELBOURNE SYDNEY AUCKLAND SINGAPORE
TOKYO IBADAN NAIROBI HARARE
GABORONE PORTSMOUTH (USA)

First published 1993

**A catalogue record for this book is
available from the British Library**

ISBN 0 435 30350 3
97 96 95 94
10 9 8 7 6 5 4 3

Designed and produced by Visual Image, Street
Cover design by Philip Parkhouse, Abingdon

Produced by Mandarin Offset
Printed and bound in China

Introduction to the series

The purpose of these books is to show what the scriptures of the six religions in the series are, to tell the story of how they grew into their present form, and to give some idea of how they are used and what they mean to believers. It is hoped that readers will be able to appreciate how important the sacred texts are to those who base their lives on them and use them to develop their faith as well as their knowledge. For this reason, members of the six major religions found in Britain today have been asked to write these books.

W. Owen Cole (Series Editor)

Acknowledgements

The Publishers would like to thank the following for permission to reproduce photographs: Ancient Art and Architecture Collection pp. 24, 25; Barnabys Picture Library p. 37; Bibliotheque Nationale pp. 12, 20; Bodleian Library, University of Oxford p. 16; Werner Braun p. 32; The Bridgeman Art Library p. 38; British Library pp. 6, 7, 11; The Hutchison Library p. 40; The Illustrated London News p. 18; Israel Postal Authority p. 8; David Jacobs, Finchley Reform Synagogue/Jewish Education Bureau pp. 30, 42; Jewish Education Bureau pp. 14, 26, 29, 35, 36, 44; © Jewish Museum, London pp. 5, 28, 34, 46; 47; By courtesy of the Memorial Scrolls Trust, London p. 39; Zefa UK p.41

The publishers would like to thank Zefa UK for permission to reproduce the cover photographs.

Contents

1 Introduction

This section tells you what this book is about.

This book is about a very special library of books written by and about the Jewish people. This vast library contains many individual books which are about ancient stories, science, history, religious ceremonies, philosophy and **ethics**. In these different books we see the unique way in which the Jews view God, humanity and the universe. No subject is excluded: birth and death; battles for power; cheating; greed; concern for the hungry and homeless; ecology; marriage and divorce; business and medical ethics.

This special treasure of the Jewish people is known as a whole as the **Torah**, a Hebrew word meaning 'teaching' or 'instruction'. The whole Torah is divided into two main sections: the Written Torah and the Oral Torah. The Written Torah is usually known as the **Tanach**, which stands for the three sub-sections: Torah, **Nevi'im** and **Ketuvim**. The Written Torah is also known in English as the Hebrew Bible or Jewish Scriptures. The Oral Torah is also known as the **Talmud** or Rabbinic Writings.

The oldest parts of the Torah were written about 3,500 years ago by many different people in different lands, but all felt that God had inspired them to write. This makes the Torah sacred, or holy. It means that God speaks to people through its pages. In this book we shall see how different groups of Jews understand the Torah. We shall also see why Jewish people still think God speaks to them when they read the Torah. Its message is for every generation, although each new generation needs to explain the Torah in its own way. Some parts of it can appear confusing or out of date. Perhaps that is why Jewish tradition suggests that a Torah student should find a teacher and some friends to share the studying.

There is an ancient Jewish story which tells of the time when God gave the Torah to the Jewish people:

> 'No bird twittered, no fowl flew, no ox bellowed...the sea did not roar, the creatures did not speak, the whole world was hushed into breathless silence.'

Another story tells of the time just before the giving of the Torah. God asked the Jewish people:

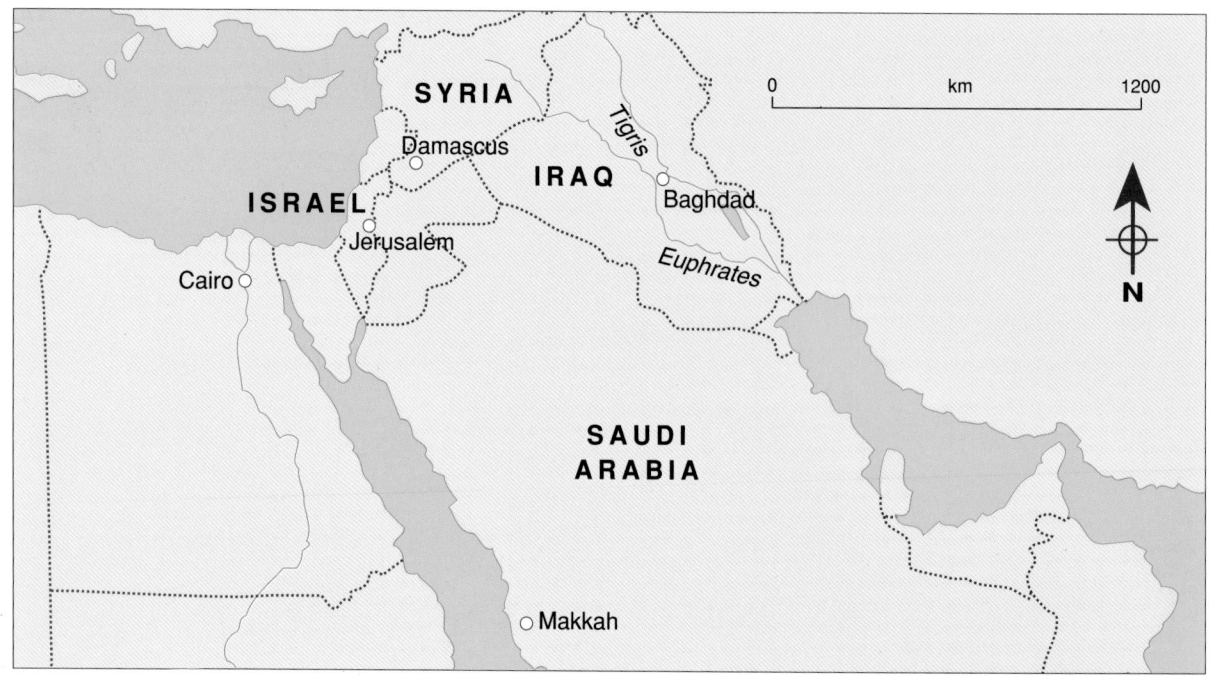

The Middle East.

'What security can you give Me so that I know that the Torah is safe in your hands?' The people responded: 'We give You our early fathers, Abraham, Isaac and Jacob.' But God refused to accept. 'What about our great prophets?' asked the people. Again God turned them down. Finally, the people said: 'We will give You our children as a guarantee.' 'That I will accept,' said God.

There is yet another interesting story that asks the question: why was the Torah given in the desert? It answers that it was given in no-man's land so that no one people or nation can claim it for itself, but all who wish to accept it can do so.

The Torah has been read, studied and interpreted over many centuries. Jews have questioned it, argued about it and, above all, loved it, for in the words of an early Jewish teacher:

'Turn it [the Torah] and turn it again, for everything you want to know is found within it.'

For the Jew, the Torah is a tree of life to all who take hold of it, and whoever holds on to it is happy. Its ways are ways of pleasantness, and all its paths lead to peace.

Miniature Torah scroll.

NEW WORDS

Ethics how we should behave

Ketuvim a Hebrew word meaning 'writings'. It includes the later books of the Tanach and books like *Psalms*

Nevi'im the books of the prophets

Talmud the collection of writings which make up the Oral Torah

Tanach a word made from the letters T (Torah), N (Nevi'im) and K, pronounced 'ch' (Ketuvim), meaning the Hebrew Bible

Torah teaching or instruction: the first five books of the Bible

FOR DISCUSSION

1 Why do you think it is important for Jews to find friends who can help them study and understand the Torah?

2 What do you think the story about silence when the Torah was given to the Jewish people means?

THINGS TO DO

1 Explain what the Jewish people meant by 'We will give You our children as a guarantee.'

2 Copy the outline of the map on page 4. Mark Egypt and Sinai on it. Why were the Jews given the Torah in the desert?

This section describes the first five books of the Hebrew Bible.

The first section of the Tanach is known as the Torah or Chumash, Hebrew for 'five', referring to the Five Books of Moses.

Jews regard Moses as the greatest and most important prophet. According to an ancient Jewish story, Moses was a shepherd who, one day, found that a young lamb was missing. Immediately he began a search. It was a very hot day, but finally, after many hours, he found the lamb, tired and thirsty.

Miriam, sister of Moses.

He gave him some water and carried him all the way back to the flock. God saw this and said:

> 'If this man can show such love for one little creature he deserves to be a leader of My flock, the people of Israel, as he will show them kindness and love.'

The Five Books of Moses are also known as the Pentateuch, the Greek word for five. The first book also has a Greek name, *Genesis*, and the Hebrew is *Beraysheet*, which means 'in the beginning'. Originally this book was called the *Book of Creation*, because it begins with an account of the creation of the universe. It also contains stories about Adam and Eve, Noah and the great flood, and tells about the beginnings of the Jewish people from the first Jews, Abraham and Sarah, to Joseph and his family in Egypt.

The second book is called *Shemot* ('names') or *Exodus*, but was originally known as the *Book of the Going out of Egypt*. It tells the story of the slavery of the Jewish people in Egypt and their liberation under Moses.

The third book is known as *Vayikra* ('He called') or *Leviticus*. The original name was the *Law of the Priests*, and much of the book concerns animal sacrifices. Another important feature of the book is the theme of holiness. The Jewish people are urged to be holy since God is holy. The fourth book,

Bemidbar ('in the wilderness') or *Numbers*, was originally given the name the *Fifth of the Musterings*, or gatherings, since it contains a census – the numbering of the Jews. It also tells of the work and special role of the Levites, the deaths of Aaron and Miriam, the brother and sister of Moses, the secret mission of the spies, and the non-Jewish prophet Balaam and his talking donkey.

The fifth book is called *Devarim* ('words') or *Deuteronomy*. The oldest name for this book was the *Repetition of the Torah*, because much of the book is a reminder of what is said in the earlier books. For example, the Ten Commandments are found in *Exodus* and then repeated, in a slightly different form, in *Deuteronomy*. The last part of the book is the farewell message and blessing of Moses before he dies.

The Five Books of Moses are regarded as the most important part of the Tanach. Each week, in **synagogues**, a section known as the sidra is read to the congregation. The cycle of readings begins with *Genesis* and ends with *Deuteronomy* twelve months later. These books are popular as well as important, because they tell about people with similar experiences and feelings to those of our own.

Title page of Genesis.

Book	Number of chapters	Number of weekly sections	Number of verses
Genesis	50	12	1,534
Exodus	40	11	1,209
Leviticus	27	10	859
Numbers	36	10	1,288
Deuteronomy	34	11	955

The Five Books of Moses.

NEW WORD

Synagogue a Greek word for a Jewish house of worship. In Hebrew it is known as Beth ha Knesset. It is also often called shul, from the German word for school

FOR DISCUSSION

1 The Chumash is a popular and important book because it is about people with similar experiences and feelings to those we have today. Do you agree or disagree?

THINGS TO DO

1 These word pairs have become jumbled. Put them in their correct pairings.

   Genesis = Shemot

   Exodus = Devarim

   Leviticus = Beraysheet

   Deuteronomy = Bemidbar

   Numbers = Vayikra

2 Write down what Chumash, Torah and Pentateuch mean. (You'll have to turn to unit 1 for one of your answers.)

3 Try to find out more about Moses. (Read *Exodus* 2 to 3:1.) Why was Moses a good man to be leader of the Jews?

3 Tanach – the prophets

This section tells you about the second part of the Hebrew Bible.

The second section of the Tanach is known as Nevi'im, the Hebrew for 'prophets'. What were prophets? Some regarded them as magicians or fortune-tellers. Others saw them as healers, while some branded them as trouble-makers.

Prophets were human beings who felt that they were messengers from God to the people. They saw many bad things and bad people in the community, and they felt the need to speak out and to urge people, especially the leaders, to change their ways and become good and kind. Prophets would never accept any form of injustice, even if the king himself was the evil-doer. As a result, some of these prophets were not very popular with the rulers, and some were thrown into prison or even killed because of the message they brought in the name of God.

Stamps of three prophets from Israel.

The prophets lived more than 25 centuries ago. They were teachers who taught all the Jewish people, from kings to the simple folk. They uttered bold statements that made people sit up and take notice. They were the conscience of the people.

This is the full list of books found in the section Nevi'im:

Joshuah	*Judges*	*1 Samuel*
2 Samuel	*1 Kings*	*2 Kings*
Isaiah	*Jeremiah*	*Ezekiel*
Hosea	*Joel*	*Amos*
Obadiah	*Jonah*	*Micah*
Nahum	*Habakkuk*	*Zephaniah*
Haggai	*Zechariah*	*Malachi*

Some of the books, like *Isaiah* and *Jeremiah*, are large works containing around 60 chapters. Other books, such as *Micah* and *Malachi*, contain only a few chapters.

Here are a few examples of their writings:

'They shall beat their swords into ploughshares and their spears into pruning hooks. Nation shall not lift up sword against nation, nor shall they practise for war any more.' (*Isaiah* 2:4 and *Micah* 4:3. Compare this with *Joel* 4:10 or 3:10 in Christian Bibles.)

These famous words can be found on the courtyard wall of the United Nations building in New York. Other examples of the prophets' sayings are:

'I desire goodness and not sacrifices, and the knowledge of God rather than burnt offerings.' (*Hosea* 6:6.)

'Let justice well up like waters and righteousness like a mighty stream.' (*Amos* 5:24.)

'This is what you, O man, have been told is good, and what the Lord asks of you: only to do justice and to love mercy and to walk humbly with your God.' (*Micah* 6:8.)

'Not by power, nor by might, but by My spirit, says the Lord of hosts.' (*Zechariah* 4:6.)

'Have we not one father? Has not one God created us? Why do we deal treacherously every person against his brother?' (*Malachi* 2:10.)

The prophets wrote warnings and also messages of hope, like this one:

'The Lord Promises New Life for Israel. The Lord says, "I will bring my people back to me. I will love them with all my heart; no longer am I angry with them. I will be to the people of Israel like rain in a dry land. They will blossom like flowers; they will be firmly rooted like the trees of Lebanon. They will be alive with new growth, and beautiful like olive-trees. They will be fragrant like the cedars of Lebanon. Once again they will live under my protection. They will grow corn and be fruitful like a vineyard. They will be as famous as the wine of Lebanon. The people of Israel will have nothing more to do with idols; I will answer their prayers and take care of them; Like an evergreen tree I will shelter them; I am the source of all their blessings."' (*Hosea* 14:4–8)

THINGS TO DO

1 Write down two or three sentences about what kinds of things mattered to the prophets.

2 Make your own notes on the kinds of things that a prophet might speak about today. Discuss your views with the rest of the class and then write an article for a newspaper called 'Modern Prophet Tells the World!'

3 a Discuss with someone else which of the examples of the prophets' writings you like best. Write it down with two reasons for liking it.

b Share your choice with the class and see which was the most popular verse.

4 Tanach – the writings

This section deals with the final part of the Hebrew Bible.

The third and final section of the Tanach is known as Ketuvim, which is Hebrew for 'writings'. The books in this section were the last to be written, and a few were nearly not included in the Scriptures, since some people felt they lacked religious inspiration.

Ketuvim contains a collection of very different books. They include hymns, proverbs and love songs. There are books which describe happy events and books which tell of sad times. The following books are contained in Ketuvim:

Psalms	Proverbs
Job	Song of Songs
Ruth	Lamentations
Ecclesiastes	Esther
Daniel	Ezra
Nehemiah	1 Chronicles
2 Chronicles	

Perhaps the best known of all these books is *Psalms*. Many of these psalms are used in services in both synagogues and churches. Tradition says that King David wrote most of the 150 psalms. This is *Psalm* 117, which is the shortest of all:

> 'O praise the Lord, all nations, praise Him, all peoples, for His love for us is great, and the truth of the Lord lasts for ever. Praise the Lord!'

Five of the books are also known as the Five Scrolls and each one is read on one of the Jewish festivals: *Ruth* (read on Shavuot); *Esther* (Purim); *Song of Songs* (**Pesach**); *Ecclesiastes* (Sukkot); *Lamentations* (read on the fast day of Tisha b'Av).

Here are a few examples from some of these books:

> 'Blessed is he who considers the poor; the Lord will deliver him in the day of evil.' (*Psalm* 41:1–2.)

> 'My child, hear the instruction of your father, and do not forsake the Torah of your mother.' (*Proverbs* 1:8.)

> 'To everything there is a season, and a time to every purpose under the heaven.' (*Ecclesiastes* 3:1.)

> '...wherever you go, I will go, where you lodge, I will lodge, your people shall be my people, and your God my God.' (*Ruth* 2:16.)

> 'For lo, the winter is past, the rain is over and gone; the flowers appear on the earth; the time of the singing bird is come, and the voice of the turtle (dove) is heard in our land.' (*Song of Songs* 2:11–12.)

> 'Go your way, eat well, and drink sweet beverages, and send portions to those for whom nothing is prepared, for this day is holy to our Lord, for the joy of the Lord is your strength.' (*Nehemiah* 8:10.)

NEW WORD

Pesach (Passover) the week-long spring festival which celebrates the freedom of the Jewish people from Egyptian slavery

FOR DISCUSSION

1 The book of *Esther* was not considered worthy by some early Jews to be included in the Bible, because the name of God is never mentioned. Do you think a story or a poem cannot be considered religious if it does not mention the name of God?

2 Discuss what the writer of *Proverbs* might have meant by 'the instruction of your father' and 'the Torah of your mother' in days when a woman's 'place' was in the home.

זה דוד המנגן בנבל "

David playing the harp.

6 The Oral Torah – the Talmud

This section tells you about the second part of the Oral Torah.

Judah and the other teachers of his time had helped the people in a new generation to understand the Torah. But then life changed even more, and the teachers and leaders found they needed to adapt some rules and add others. Their new writings included proverbs and **parables**, facts of science and medicine, even humorous sketches. All this finally developed into a very large work which they called the Gemara, which means 'completion'. Together with the Mishnah, the combined work was called Talmud, which means 'study'.

The Talmud is like a huge encyclopædia, containing two and a half million words; it

A page from the Talmud. The text includes A: the title of the book (Kiddushin) which is mainly about marriage; B: the first word of the text; C: Mishnah text; D: Gemara text; E: the commentary of Rashi; F: marginal notes and commentaries.

14

took almost 800 years to complete. Here is a small selection of interesting statements from the Talmud:

'It takes 24 hours for the earth to revolve around the sun.'

'When the clouds are bright, they contain little water.'

'Curly-headed people should not be cashiers, as they may be suspected of concealing coins in their hair.'

'A blow, though it may not cause bleeding, may cause a blood clot.'

'The health of the body depends on the teeth.'

'Those who eat food with unwashed hands endanger their health because hands are full of dangerous germs.'

'A properly balanced diet, avoidance of overeating and attention to the calls of nature on time, prevent intestinal trouble.'

'Before the Flood [of Noah] human beings were vegetarians.'

'Breakfast is the most important meal of the day.'

'One is not permitted to eat until one has fed one's animals.'

'Whether Jew or non-Jew, man or woman, rich or poor, it is according to deeds that God's presence descends.'

'Charity knows neither race nor creed.'

'If someone says you have the ears of an ass, pay no attention; but if two tell you that, get yourself a saddle.'

'A young Talmud student asked his teacher to make him a **rabbi**, a Jewish teacher. He was tested with the question: "What would you do if a man cut his hand on the Shabbat and began to bleed heavily?" The student answered: "Wait a moment while I look it up in the Talmud." "Never mind," said his teacher. "Go and continue your studies. By the time you looked it up the poor man would have bled to death!"'

More than 2,000 teachers are mentioned in the Talmud. Many of them had humble jobs such as shoe-makers, farmers, sandal-makers, bakers and carpenters. Through their efforts the Talmud has become an important book for Jewish people. Indeed, after the Tanach, the Talmud has become the greatest landmark in Judaism. Long ago, some Jewish teachers felt that the Talmud was as holy as the Five Books of Moses. They even said that when Moses was on Mount Sinai he received from God not only the Written Torah, but also the Oral Torah, the Talmud.

NEW WORDS

Parables stories which teach a moral lesson

Rabbi the spiritual leader of a synagogue who conducts services, teaches adults and children, and has other duties similar to a Minister in other religions

FOR DISCUSSION

1 Discuss each of the statements from the Talmud to make sure that you understand them.

THINGS TO DO

1 The Talmud was completed about 1,500 years ago. Which statement from it surprised you most? Give reasons for your choice.

2 Which pieces of advice are most helpful for life in today's world?

This section tells you about early groups and their attitude to the Torah.

Since the books of the Torah were written by different people in different lands during different ages, it should not be too surprising that people would develop different ideas about God and how best to serve Him. In the early history of the Jewish people, three groups emerged. All three groups claimed to follow and accept the Torah, but as we shall see, each viewed the Torah in a different way.

Samaritans

The Samaritans have a history that dates back to the 7th century BCE and have always lived

*A Samaritan, originally published in the **Illustrated** London News on 18 December 1869.*

in Nablus, the Biblical Shechem. Although they do not consider themselves Jews, they have adopted a form of Judaism based on the Five Books of Moses alone, rejecting all other books of the Tanach. They also offer up animal sacrifices on the festival of Pesach (Passover) on their holy mountain, Gerizim. Although Jews also used to offer up animal sacrifices, this stopped when their Temple in Jerusalem was destroyed by the Romans in 70CE.

Like their cousins, the Jews, Samaritans observe the Shabbat and festivals, practise **circumcision** and believe in the coming of a **Messiah**. They also put a **mezuzah** on their door, though it does not contain the **shema**, but a shortened form of the Ten Commandments. Their Hebrew writing and pronunciation is probably how very ancient Hebrew looked and sounded. The community today consists of about 500 people.

Sadducees

The Sadducees were both a religious and a political group. Their membership came mainly from the priestly community. They accepted the whole of the Tanach, but rejected the Oral Torah. They interpreted the Tanach in a very literal way. Since most of them were priests, they saw themselves as superior to other people. They followed their own calendar and rejected certain beliefs, such as life after death. When the Temple was destroyed, many of them no longer had a job to do, because they were priests, and so not long after, they disappeared as a distinct group.

Pharisees

The Pharisees were also a religious and political group, but unlike the Sadducees, they gained members from the ordinary people. They believed that Judaism must develop and even move with the times, so they helped to create the Oral Torah. They were keen to bring to the people new rituals and ceremonies, but they also wished to build up ethical and moral ideas. They helped make Judaism a religion centred on the home rather than on the Temple. They encouraged the setting up of synagogues and schools all over the country. They liberalized Torah laws and were often willing to adapt and change laws so that they would be more meaningful and understandable for their time. For example, they taught that the Shabbat had been given to the people, not the people to the Shabbat, and therefore advised:

> '**Desecrate** the Shabbat and extinguish a man-made candle, rather than let a soul, a God-made candle, be extinguished.'

The Pharisees made Torah study available for all the people, not just a selected few. In short, the popular Pharisees made the Torah of Israel available for the entire people of Israel.

NEW WORDS

Circumcision cutting off the foreskin; a ritual which is practised on all Jewish baby boys

Desecrate break or disobey a sacred occasion, place or ritual

Messiah a human being chosen by God to usher in peace for the Jewish people and all the world

Mezuzah (plural mezuzot) a parchment scroll which is placed in a small case and fixed to the doorposts of Jewish homes

Shema one of the most important Jewish prayers, recited every morning and evening

THINGS TO DO

1 List the main differences between Jews and Samaritans. You might like to do this in a table.

2 Why did the Sadducees disappear in 70CE?

3 Why do you think Judaism largely owed its survival after 70CE to the work of the Pharisees? Give reasons.

10 Later Torah teachers

This section is about Torah teachers of the Middle Ages.

In every generation there have been teachers of the Torah, and during the Middle Ages the following scholars flourished. We call them commentators, since they comment on the Torah and offer insight and meanings into the text.

Rashi (1040–1105)

Rashi is an abbreviation of Rabbi Shlomo (Solomon) ben (son of) Yitzchaki (Isaac), who was born in Troyes, France. He earned his living as a grape-grower, and Troyes was a city famous for its wine. As a young man Rashi was sent to centres in France and Germany to study the Torah with great rabbis, after which he opened his own Torah school. During these years he wrote by hand commentaries on every sentence in the Torah. These commentaries acted like a magic key, for his explanations unlocked meanings and ideas, and helped answer the many questions of his students, such as: 'Why does the Torah begin with the story of creation?' or 'Why did God ask Noah to build an ark?' Rashi had three daughters, and although in those days it was not usual for girls to study the Torah, he taught his daughters. They, too, asked him many questions, so his commentaries were in many ways answers to his own daughters' queries.

Rashi would compose his sentences with a quill pen dipped in ink on paper, which was dried with grains of sand. After the invention of printing, the first Hebrew book that was printed appeared in Italy in 1475, and it consisted of the Hebrew Bible with Rashi's commentary. His commentary became very popular because of his manner of explaining difficult words and phrases in a simple way. Rashi used many French words to explain sections of the Torah, and this can be useful to French students tracing old French terms. His commentary was translated into Latin and became helpful to Christians, as well as to Jews. No wonder Rashi earned the special title of Supreme Commentator.

Here are some of Rashi's sayings:

> Customs of later generations are Torah.
>
> Who rears his son to be righteous is like an immortal.
> > (commentary to *Genesis* 18:19)
>
> Be sure to ask your teacher his reasons and sources.
>
> It is better to listen to one who is lenient and permits, for anybody can be strict and forbid.
>
> Teachers learn from their students' discussions.
> > (commentary to *Proverbs* 13:23)
>
> Study in joy and good cheer, in accordance with your intelligence and heart's dictates.
>
> In the context of his own generation, Noah was considered righteous, but had he lived in the generation of Abraham, he would not have been considered as important.
> > (commentary to *Genesis* 6:9)

Abraham ibn Ezra (1090–1164)

Abraham ibn Ezra was born in Spain during the period which Jews call the Golden Age of Judaism. This was because, at that time, Spain was under Muslim rule, and like their cousins the Jews, Muslims also loved learning. Abraham ibn Ezra was a brilliant writer. He not only wrote a commentary on the Hebrew Bible, but also wrote books on grammar, astronomy and poems on almost every subject imaginable. He was fond of playing with words and rhymes and wrote with a fine sense of humour.

All of Abraham ibn Ezra's books were written in Arabic, since both Muslims and Jews in Spain spoke the language. He decided, however, that since Jews in other countries could not understand Arabic he would translate them into Hebrew. Many years later, Christopher Columbus used his

Out of Luck

Twas sure a luckless planet that ruled when I was born,
I hoped for fame and fortune, I have but loss and scorn.
An evil fate pursues me with unrelenting spite.
If I sold lamps and candles, the sun would shine all night.
I cannot, cannot prosper, no matter what I try.
Were selling shrouds my business, no man would ever die!

A poem, in English translation, by Abraham ibn Ezra.

books and maps during his voyage to America.

Abraham ibn Ezra was a restless person and spent much time in travelling to other countries. In 1158 he visited London, and even managed to reach India, writing some of his 100 books on the way. It is also said that he created a golem – a Jewish version of Frankenstein's monster, or a zombie. Perhaps he thought this artificial person would wait on him while he wrote his books.

FOR DISCUSSION

1 Why might Christians be instructed in the writings of Rashi and other Jewish scholars?

THINGS TO DO

1 Write an up-to-date version of ibn Ezra's poem, 'Out of Luck'.

2 Why do you think that the first books to be printed were often scriptures?

This section tells you about the discovery of the Dead Sea Scrolls.

Many people dream of finding a treasure. This is the true story of a **Bedouin** boy who did find a treasure – in the middle of a desert!

In the spring of 1947, a young Bedouin boy was getting hot and bothered, because for hours he had been climbing around the cliffs near the Dead Sea looking for his lost goat. Feeling a little tired, he stopped to rest on a ledge and found himself opposite a cave. He thought that perhaps the goat could be in there. He threw in a small stone, but no goat came running out. Instead, he heard the sound of pottery breaking. He was very

puzzled. What was pottery doing in an empty cave in the middle of the desert? He hurried to get the adult members of his family and on entering the cave they found eight tall clay jars. Inside each one was a rolled scroll with unfamiliar writing. They realized that these scrolls were very old. Before long, they sold the scrolls.

Eventually more scrolls were discovered at Qumran, the Arabic name for the area. They were studied and then displayed in the Museum of the Hebrew University in Jerusalem. The scrolls have the text, in whole or in part, of all the books of the Tanach, except the book of *Esther*. They go back 1,000 years more than previously known

The cave where the Dead Sea Scrolls were found in Qumran.

Dead Sea Scroll fragment.

copies. There were other writings, such as a manual laying down a strict order of discipline for members of this community, known as **Essenes**, who were a Jewish group who wished to live in the desert and follow a simple life and the laws of ritual purity.

Why were these scrolls hidden in the first place? Probably to save them from falling into the hands of their enemies when the Essene settlement was destroyed by Romans in 70CE. Another question to be asked is: how was it possible for the scrolls to be preserved for almost 2,000 years? Desert areas receive very little rain, so the climate is very dry. A cool, dark cave helped to keep the scrolls at the right temperature, and, left undisturbed, they survived. They have given scholars a lot of important information about Biblical texts and how the Qumran sect lived all those centuries ago.

If you visit Israel you will be able to see the scrolls, which are housed in a building called the Shrine of the Book. This is all thanks to a young Bedouin who, by the way, never did find his goat!

NEW WORDS

Bedouin an Arab of the desert, who often wanders around

Essenes a Jewish group which helped to write and preserve the Dead Sea Scrolls

FOR DISCUSSION

1 Look back to unit 4. Why might the Qumran community not have used the book of *Esther*?

2 Visitors to the Shrine of the Book have to switch on a light to view the scrolls. After a few minutes the light goes off. What do you think is the reason for this?

THINGS TO DO

1 Give reasons why scholars were excited when the Dead Sea Scrolls were found.

This section tells you how Jews today view the Torah.

There have always been differences of opinion between Jews. Although all religious Jews consider the Torah their most important guide to life, they view it in different ways. Some see it as written by God, while others accept that human beings have written it. The former view is held by Jews who are called Orthodox or traditional, while the latter view is held by Jews who call themselves Progressive, Reform, or Liberal.

Orthodox Jews firmly believe that the Torah is of Divine origin, that every word in it is true, and that it comes directly from God and was written down by Moses on God's instruction. Since it is directly from God, the Torah must be perfect and unchanging. The message is the same for all generations and nothing can be changed, deleted or added. God has revealed Himself through the Torah, and if God is perfect, so is the Torah.

Moses is seen as a human being, but he is regarded as the perfect secretary, writing down every word and even every letter, correctly, and therefore making no mistakes from beginning to end.

Orthodox Jews assert that the Torah has not been changed because it has been guarded most preciously in all generations and has not left the possession of Jews even during times of persecution. They believe that it is wrong of people to neglect some of the

Interior of a Progressive synagogue.

Torah

laws, relying on their own wisdom to decide which they should obey and which they can ignore. To Orthodox Jews, it is wrong to compare human wisdom with God's wisdom, by observing only the laws which their limited reasoning can accept. The Torah was given on Mount Sinai 31 centuries ago, and every law and commandment is binding on all Jews, they say: all laws are equal in importance. So, for example, the observance of the **kosher** laws are equal to the commandment of loving one's neighbour.

Progressive Jews believe that the Torah is the word of God, as understood by human beings. It was written by various law-givers and prophets who were children of their age, and whose knowledge was limited to the period in which they lived. These inspired people wrote down what they thought were the words from God, but being mere humans, they were liable to make mistakes or write about certain ideas which, although right for their own generation, would not be considered right by later generations.

Progressive Jews, therefore, feel that some beliefs and practices are no longer relevant, and should no longer be observed, while other laws should be kept by every generation. Decisions about whether to follow other practices, they argue, should be left to the conscience of the individual. For example, some Progressive Jews feel that all the kosher laws should be kept. Like their Orthodox friends, they will refrain from eating food such as pork or shellfish, and they will not eat meat and dairy produce in the same meal. They will also get their meat from a kosher butcher. Other Progressive Jews will refrain from eating forbidden foods, but will buy meat from an ordinary butcher or a supermarket, and will not wait an interval before having a dairy product after a meat meal. There will be others who feel that the kosher laws no longer have any religious significance.

Both Orthodox and Progressive Jews claim that they observe the Shabbat. Strictly Orthodox Jews can only get to their synagogue by walking, since taking the car or going by public transport is considered to be breaking the Shabbat. If you live too far away from a synagogue, they say, it is better to pray on your own at home than break the Shabbat. Progressive Jews have no objections to using a car or public transport on the Shabbat. Better to come, they say, than not to come. So car parks belonging to Progressive synagogues are open on the Shabbat, while Orthodox synagogue ones are closed.

Differences between Orthodox and Progressive viewpoints are very important, but the common ground held by all Jews is more important, since both groups show great respect to their sacred book, the Torah, even if it is in different ways.

NEW WORD

Kosher a Hebrew word meaning 'fit'. According to the Torah, Jews can only eat kosher animals, that is animals that have split hooves and chew the cud, such as the ox or goat, but not the pig or rabbit. For a full list of kosher animals, fish and birds, see chapter 11 of the book of *Leviticus*

FOR DISCUSSION

1 An Orthodox Jew might argue that if you neglect one part of the Torah you'll end up ignoring all of it. Discuss this view.

2 Why do you think some Jews are Progressive and others Orthodox?

THINGS TO DO

1 List the differences between Orthodox and Progressive Jews. Use a table like this:

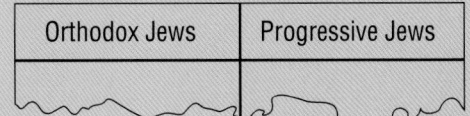

Orthodox Jews	Progressive Jews

2 Do you think Orthodox and Progressive Jews have more in common with one another or more differences? Give reasons.

13 The dressed Torah

This section tells you about the various ornaments placed on the Torah.

In synagogues, the Five Books of Moses are in a scroll known as a Sefer Torah or Torah scroll. Since the Torah is considered the holiest object in Judaism, it is natural that it is adorned or dressed with beautiful ornaments. While these objects can never be more important than the scroll itself, synagogue members are always prepared to spend money on beautiful adornments, because most of the time scrolls will be dressed and they are only undressed when being read.

A well dressed Torah scroll will have the following items.

Rimmonim with bells.

Mantle

A mantle can be made from various textiles. The function of the mantle is both to protect the scroll and to beautify it. It can be in various colours, but blue and maroon are the most popular. However, all synagogues use white during the festivals of **Rosh Hashanah** (New Year) and **Yom Kippur** (Day of Atonement).

Mantles are embroidered by hand or by machine using symbols, usually from the Tanach, such as the Ten Commandments, lions or crowns. Sometimes the name of the individual or family who presented the mantle is embroidered on the bottom of it.

Binder

After a Torah scroll is rolled up and before the mantle is placed over it, the scroll is bound with a length of material two or three inches wide. This holds the scroll tightly. In the Middle Ages these binders were beautifully decorated, often with verses from the Hebrew Bible or with scenes from Jewish life, such as a wedding. Today, most binders are plain.

Crown

The Talmud speaks about three crowns: the crown of priesthood, connected with Aaron and his priestly descendants; the crown of kingship, connected with King David; and the crown of the Torah, which any ordinary Jew who studies the Torah can attain. There is a fourth crown, which is even more important: the crown of a good name.

Most Torah scrolls are dressed with two narrow units, which are placed on the wooden rollers at each end of the scroll. These are called rimmonim, meaning 'pomegranates' in Hebrew. Some scrolls have a single unit crown placed over the rollers. In both cases, the material is made of silver and often has beautiful designs.

Breastplate

A breastplate is placed on a Torah scroll as a reminder of the gold breastplate worn by the High Priest when the Temple in Jerusalem existed. Today, it is usually made of silver and measures about eight by ten inches. A chain is attached so that it can be draped over the two rollers.

Pointer

The pointer is known in Hebrew as a yad, which means 'hand'. It is used to point to the words of the Torah when it is being read. A yad is usually made of silver, but it could also be made of other materials, such as wood or ivory.

The yad is about six to eight inches long. At its end there is a sculpted hand with the index finger extended. This is used to avoid touching the scroll with a human hand, since the scroll is regarded as sacred. A finger can also act as an eraser, and in time will rub out letters or even words. This would make the scroll unfit for use until it had been restored by a scribe.

So far we have looked at the Torah scroll in use among Jews who originally come from Central or Eastern Europe. They are called Ashkenasim. Jews who are originally from Spain and Portugal are known as Sephardim. Here, Torah scrolls are placed in cylindrical metal or wooden boxes, lined with velvet. These containers are often highly decorated and stand vertically and, when opened, reveal the scroll. Although nobody is sure why Sephardim put their scrolls in containers, it is probably because these countries have hot, dry climates which could damage the scrolls unless they are well protected.

A number of dressed Torah scrolls.

FOR DISCUSSION

1 Scrolls are dressed in a beautiful way to give honour to the Torah, but not to worship it. Do you think honour can be shown without the need to spend much money on such items?

THINGS TO DO

1 Copy or trace one of the dressed Torah scrolls. Mark the mantle, crown and breastplate.

2 Write a letter from a Jew to a non-Jewish friend explaining why you think it is important to dress the Torah.

3 Make your own scroll and decorate it. Write a verse from the Tanach inside it. (You could pick one from unit 3 if you have difficulty in choosing one.)

NEW WORDS

Rosh Hashanah the Jewish New Year, which is celebrated in September or October

Yom Kippur a fast day which takes place nine days after Rosh Hashanah

14 The undressed Torah

This section is about reading from the Torah scroll.

Most of the time a Torah scroll is covered or dressed. Indeed, it shows a lack of respect and honour to have a scroll undressed, except when someone is about to read from it. Readings from a Torah scroll take place during the morning and afternoon services of the Shabbat and some festivals, and also on Monday and Thursday mornings. These days were market days in ancient Israel, and synagogues could be sure of good attendances, so this was when the Torah was read. One scroll is used on most Sabbaths and

Woman carrying a Torah scroll.

weekdays, but on festivals and a few Sabbaths two scrolls are used. The scroll is paraded around the synagogue, with people bowing before it as one would before a monarch. Some people kiss the mantle with the fringes of their **tallit** (prayer shawl). The scroll is then undressed, often by children.

A number of people are 'called up' during the Torah reading. On the Shabbat, in Orthodox synagogues, seven people are usually called up. In Progressive synagogues the number is usually between one and three. Centuries ago, any person who was able was allowed to read from the Torah. This included women. However, later tradition decided that because of the 'dignity of the congregation' only men would be called up. It was felt by some that the presence of women would be distracting for men. This custom continues among Orthodox congregations, but Progressive synagogues have returned to the earlier practice. Another early custom was for everyone called up to read their portion from the Torah. However, since some people read better than others, it was decided not to embarrass the poor readers. So instead a special Torah reader was appointed, called the baal koray ('master of the reading'), to read on behalf of everyone. This practice continues in almost every synagogue. Every person, however, is expected to chant or read the blessings before and after the reading.

After the Torah reading, the scroll is raised and the text is shown to the congregation, who sing:

> 'This is the Torah which Moses placed before the people of Israel, according to the commandment of God, by the hand of Moses.'

Some people also add:

> 'Moses commanded us the Torah, the heritage of the community of Jacob.'

There then follows the second reading, usually taken from the Prophets, known as the haftarah ('concluding reading'). It is read or chanted from a printed book.

Blessings before the Torah reading:

> Reader: 'Praise the Lord Who is to be praised.'
>
> Congregation, then repeated by reader: 'Praised be the Lord Who is praised for ever and ever.'
>
> Reader: 'Praised are You, Lord our God, Ruler of the universe, Who chose us from all peoples and has given us Your Torah. Praised are You, Lord, Giver of the Torah.'

Blessings after the Torah reading:

> Reader: 'Praised are You, Lord our God, Ruler of the universe, Who has given us a Torah of truth, and planted within us eternal life. Praised are You, Lord, Giver of the Torah.'

Blessings before the haftarah reading:

> Reader: 'Praised are You, Lord our God, Ruler of the universe, Who chose good prophets and was pleased by their words which were spoken in truth. Praised are You, Lord, Who chooses the Torah, Moses His servant, Israel His people, and the true and righteous prophets.'

Blessings after the haftarah reading:

> Reader: 'For the Torah, for the worship, for the prophets, and for this Shabbat day which You gave us, Lord our God, for holiness and rest, for glory and beauty. We thank and praise You, Lord our God, for all things may Your name be praised by every living thing. Praised are You, Lord, Who makes the Shabbat holy.'

Plan of an Orthodox synagogue.

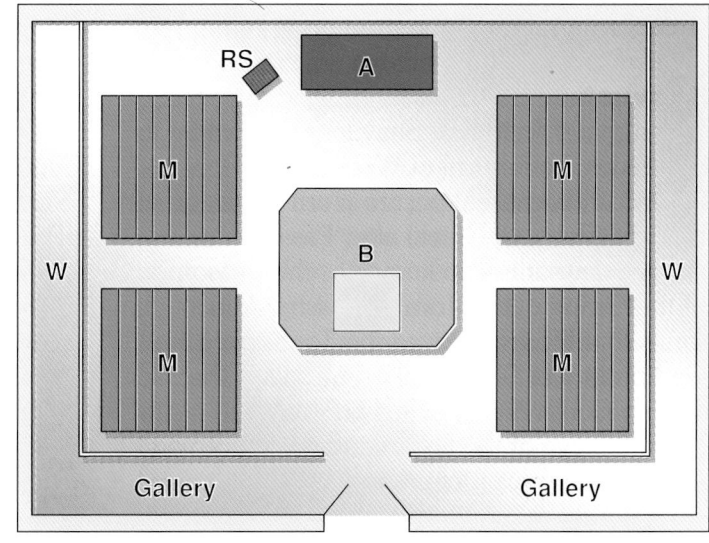

A	Ark	**M**	Seats for men and boys
RS	Rabbi's seat	**W**	Seats for women and girls
B	Bimah		

NEW WORD

Tallit a four-cornered prayer shawl worn by male worshippers at morning services. In some Progressive synagogues, women also wear them

FOR DISCUSSION

1 Why do you think a number of people are called up to read the scroll at a Shabbat service?

THINGS TO DO

1 Look back to the table of differences between Orthodox and Progressive Jews which you made in unit 12. Add any further differences from this unit.

2 How do Jews show respect for the Torah when it is carried among the congregation?

3 Write a letter from a Jew explaining how people's actions when a Torah is carried among the congregation show respect for it.

16 Torah in Jewish symbols

This section tells you about two objects connected with the Torah.

Symbols are a kind of visual aid which can be very helpful. Jewish symbols can help show the vitality of Judaism. Two important objects

for Jews, often known as the 'outward signs', have the Torah in them.

Mezuzah

If you look carefully, you can normally recognize a Jewish house by a mezuzah. A mezuzah is a small parchment, with 22 lines from the book of *Deuteronomy*, chapter 6, verses 4 to 9, and chapter 11, verses 13 to 21. These verses are handwritten by a scribe and form the watchword of faith for the Jewish people – the belief in one God:

> 'Hear, O Israel, the Lord is our God, the Lord is One.'

The piece of parchment is carefully rolled up and then placed into a small case, which can be made of plastic, metal or wood. It is fixed on the upper third of the right doorpost, its top slanting slightly inward. Two nails are used to fix it.

A mezuzah (plural mezuzot) is usually placed on all doors of a Jewish house with the exception of the bathroom and toilet. It remains a constant reminder to those who live in the house and to visitors that this is a Jewish home. Although a mezuzah must never be regarded as a good luck symbol, it is considered to be a badge of honour and a beautiful symbol of Jewish living.

On entering or leaving a Jewish house, very Orthodox Jews will kiss their fingers and then touch the mezuzah, reciting the words:

> 'May God keep my going out and my coming in from now on and for ever more.'

Tephilin

When an Orthodox boy becomes a **Bar Mitzvah**, he is expected to put on **tephilin** every day, except on a Shabbat or festival. This can be done on his own at home, before leaving for school or work, or at the early morning service, around 7.30am, at the local synagogue.

Tephilin consist of two cube-shaped boxes, about one cubic inch in size. Like a mezuzah,

A 15th century Italian ivory-cased mezuzah.

Bar Mitzvah boy holding a Torah scroll and wearing tephilin.

placed on the forehead. The arm box has all the above verses on one parchment scroll. The box which is placed on the forehead has the same verses but they are divided into four separate parchment scrolls, which are then placed into four separate compartments within the box.

The tephilin of the head is a reminder for the Jews to direct their thoughts and minds to God. The tephilin of the arm is placed near the heart to remind Jews to be sincere in service to God. Before and after use, the tephilin are kissed and blessings are recited. Although for many centuries tephilin boxes have been black, in the past other colours except red were allowed, especially blue or purple.

Women are not expected to wear tephilin, but in past centuries some very saintly women have worn them and a few women wear them today. Very few Progressive Jews wear tephilin.

According to the Midrash, God Himself wears tephilin. In the Jew's tephilin it is written:

> 'You are One and Your Name is One.'

In God's pair of tephilin it says:

> 'There is none like Your people Israel, a unique people on earth.'

both boxes contain the verses from *Deuteronomy*. These verses also appear in the prayerbook and are known as the shema, from the first word, 'hear' or 'listen'. In addition, tephilin boxes contain verses from *Exodus*, chapter 13, verses 1 to 10 and 11 to 16. One box is placed on the left arm, the arm nearest the heart, and the strap is twined seven times around the arm; the other box is

NEW WORDS

Bar Mitzvah a 'son of the commandment'; a thirteen-year-old boy who is accepted as a religious adult

Tephilin the two small leather boxes and straps worn at all morning services except Sabbath and festivals

FOR DISCUSSION

1 How do symbols like tephilin and mezuzot help Jews to keep their faith?

2 Discuss the value of birthday cards, holiday snapshots and videos and presents brought back from holidays for keeping friendships alive.

THINGS TO DO

1 If you were a Jew, how might tephilin help you when you pray?

2 What thoughts might go through a Jew's mind as he or she touches a mezuzah before entering the house?

This section looks at the work of the Torah scribe.

It would be rather strange if we went into a bookshop or library and were offered a book that was handwritten rather than printed. Modern homes have word processors or typewriters. It seems that the only handwritten work done today is at school and for homework!

Among Jews, however, the Torah scroll is always handwritten. It is not written on paper but on vellum or parchment from a kosher animal skin. Only a very expert person can write a Torah scroll. He is called a **sofer**, a Hebrew word meaning 'scribe'. It takes about seven years of training to become a qualified sofer, and it takes a year or more to write a whole Torah scroll.

A sofer uses a quill pen made with five feathers of a kosher bird, such as the goose or turkey. He makes a very black ink, usually by blending gall nuts, copper sulphate crystals, gum arabic and water. Scribes work under great pressure, and, being human, can make mistakes. Most can be corrected by erasing the ink with a knife and a pumice stone. However, if the error is one of the names of God, this must not be rubbed out. Instead, the faulty piece of parchment is cut out and buried in a Jewish cemetery. Scribes must concentrate fully and are not supposed to talk while writing. Many scribes work for four hours before resting. If they finish at night they do not go to sleep until the ink dries.

A sofer needs 60 to 80 pieces of parchment, each of which has 248 columns of writing, to complete a scroll. Then he and

A scribe at work.

Where the Torah is kept, in an Italian synagogue in Jerusalem.

other learned Jews must check and recheck the entire text. Only then can the scroll be considered fit for use. After the checks, the parchment pieces will be sewn into a scroll. Finally each side of the scroll must be sewn onto a wooden handle before the scroll is ready to be used.

No animal can be killed just for its skin. Only if an animal was killed for food or died of natural causes can its hide be used to make parchment. Torah scrolls must also be checked every few years to make sure all the words and letters are still clear, otherwise a sofer must rewrite these letters or words.

When a scroll can no longer be used because of old age, it is buried in a Jewish cemetery.

The sofer is a skilled artist, but also a religious Jew. Today our society relies on machines for almost all areas of life. No machine, however, can do the work of a scribe, since the Torah scroll can only be created by human and loving hands.

NEW WORD

Sofer a Jewish scribe who writes Torah scrolls and mezuzot (plural for mezuzah) by hand

THINGS TO DO

1 How does the work of a scribe show the importance of the Torah?

2 Explain why it takes seven years to qualify as a scribe.

3 Give reasons why Torah scrolls have to be handwritten. Why wouldn't a synagogue use a printed book?

18 The sad Torah

This section looks at when Jews and their Torah have been attacked and destroyed.

It has not been easy to be a Jew in many parts of the world. In past centuries Jews have been attacked, tortured, expelled and even killed. Their holy books have not escaped criticism, either. In 13th century France, for instance, countless copies of the Talmud were publicly burned. This was mainly because some Christians incorrectly believed that the Talmud attacks the Christian religion.

The burning of the Talmud, painted by Pedro Berruguete in the 15th century.

Nazi persecution

When the Nazis swept to power in Germany in the 1930s, they too attacked Jewish people and Jewish buildings. Many synagogues were set on fire, and Torah scrolls also ended up being burned, unless members of the congregation were able to rescue them.

The Nazis sought to destroy all those whom they regarded as their enemies. Most of these people perished in the infamous concentration and extermination camps. Among them were six million Jews. The Nazis intended to set up a museum about the Jewish people, so they gathered together ornaments, books and Torah scrolls. Thankfully, the Nazis were defeated and the nightmare in Europe and elsewhere ended. Much of the material the Nazis had gathered together was found in Prague, and was taken over by the state Jewish Museum of Prague, except for the Torah scrolls, which lay piled in a disused synagogue for more than 20 years. In 1964, these 'sad' scrolls, 1,564 in number, were brought to the Westminster Synagogue in London, where they were individually numbered, inspected and catalogued. Many of them were in poor condition; others could be restored so that they could once again be used in synagogues. These restored scrolls can now be found in synagogues throughout the world. They are on permanent loan. Each scroll bears a brass tablet with a number corresponding to the number on a certificate, which describes the origin of the scroll and any known particulars.

It is good to know that these scrolls still live and are a witness to the many Jews who died during the period Jews call the **Holocaust**.

'Sad' Torah scrolls saved from the Holocaust.

NEW WORD

Holocaust the murder of six million Jews by the Nazis during the Second World War

THINGS TO DO

1 Why might a synagogue feel honoured to be lent a sad Torah scroll?

2 Write a paragraph for your local paper about a sad Torah scroll which has just been lent to the local synagogue.

3 Imagine you are a Sad Torah scroll. Tell your story from being in a synagogue in Austria in 1937 to arriving in a London synagogue in 1964.

4 If you have the opportunity to make a school visit to a synagogue, ask if they have one of the Sad Torah scrolls and perhaps you will be told a little of the history of that scroll.

20 The teenager's Torah

This section tells you how the Torah affects young Jewish people.

Bar Mitzvah

In some countries you become an adult at 21. In others the age is eighteen. Among Jews the age is thirteen years and one day for boys, and twelve years and one day for girls. Becoming an adult in Judaism means taking on the responsibility of observing the commandments of the Torah. For boys this means putting on tephilin and being counted for the **minyan**, the quorum of ten males needed for public worship. It is also the opportunity for boys to read from the Torah for the first time before the congregation. Of course, this will entail much preparation, which will include several years in a Religion

A Bat Mitzvah girl.

School and a final year of extra work on the Torah reading itself. After much hard work, a boy will become a Bar Mitzvah, a son of the commandment. Although a Bar Mitzvah is considered to be an adult in the religious sense, obviously a thirteen-year-old will still continue to grow and mature and continue to attend school! He will remain a minor and still depend on his parents for food, clothing and, of course, pocket money!

Although having a Bar Mitzvah ceremony is still a very popular tradition, there is no mention of it anywhere in the Torah. The only clue is one statement in the Talmud:

'Thirteen is the age for the fulfilment of the commandments.'

It took many centuries before the Bar Mitzvah ceremony as it is held today took root.

A Bar Mitzvah will sing or read the blessings before and after his Torah reading, which will be part of the sidra (weekly Shabbat portion). He will also read the haftarah (reading from the Prophets), together with blessings before and after. He will probably give a short account of what his reading is all about. In some synagogues he will also be expected to conduct almost the entire service. The rabbi will address him and present him with a book, often a prayerbook, and perhaps a Bar Mitzvah certificate. He will also receive a blessing.

Bat Mitzvah

Until this century, there was no ceremony for girls reaching the age of twelve. Today most synagogues have the ceremony of **Bat Mitzvah** (daughter of the commandment) or Bat Hayill (daughter of worth). In Orthodox synagogues the ceremony usually takes place on a Sunday afternoon, often with a group of girls together. They will read a passage from the Hebrew Bible or prayerbook but not from the Torah scroll. In Progressive synagogues, the ceremony will be identical to a Bar Mitzvah, even held when the girl is at the same age, thirteen.

After the ceremony in the synagogue, the parents of the Bar Mitzvah or Bat Mitzvah will invite their relatives and friends to a party. Sometimes this will be in the form of a lunch after the service, or dinner on Sunday evening. The Bar or Bat Mitzvah will give a speech thanking everyone for coming and for their presents.

So Judaism honours its teenagers by allowing them to read from the Torah on the occasion of their Bar or Bat Mitzvah.

Some Progressive synagogues have an additional ceremony for young people when they reach the age of fifteen or sixteen. This is known as Kabbalat Torah (acceptance of the Torah). See unit 15 for more information.

NEW WORDS

Minyan a quorum – the minimum number of males over the age of thirteen (Orthodox) and females (Progressive) needed for public or congregational worship

Bat Mitzvah a 'daughter of the commandment'; a twelve-year-old girl who is accepted as a religious adult

FOR DISCUSSION

1 Is it as important to have a special Bat Mitzvah ceremony for girls as it is to have a Bar Mitzvah for boys? Why or why not?

THINGS TO DO

1 In practice, what does it mean for a Jewish teenager to become a religious adult?

2 Prepare a Bat Mitzvah and Bar Mitzvah training course. What should it include? Should there be different elements for boys and girls? If so, why?

21 The universal Torah

This section tells you how the Torah is for both Jews and non-Jews.

According to Jewish tradition, there are 613 commandments in the Torah. Of these, 365 are negative ('You shall not'), which matches the number of days in the year, and 248 are positive ('You shall'), corresponding to the number of bones in the human body. No one can keep all the commandments. Some cannot be kept because they are concerned with the Temple, which has not existed for 2,000 years. Young people under the age of thirteen and women do not have to observe a great number of commandments.

One rabbi in the Talmud taught that various prophets came and reduced the number of commandments. So David, according to Psalm 15, reduced them to only eleven. Then came Isaiah who, according to *Isaiah 33*, reduced them to six. Next came Micah, who halved them to three (*Micah* 6:8). Isaiah returned and reduced them to two, namely:

▌ 'Keep judgement and do righteousness.' ▐

Finally, two prophets came and reduced them to one. First Amos:

▌ 'See Me and live.' (*Amos* 5:4.) ▐

Zodiac symbol of the Hebrew third month of Sivan.

SIVAN   סיון

TWINS   תאומים

Then Habakkuk:

'The righteous shall live by His faith.'
(*Habakkuk* 2:4.)

Although not many non-Jews have heard of the 613 commandments, most have heard about the Ten Commandments. Indeed, among Christians the Ten Commandments are as important as they are among Jews. Jewish tradition refers to them as the Ten Sayings, as the Hebrew Bible contains two versions, one in *Exodus* 34 and the other slightly different version in *Deuteronomy* 10. Here are the Ten Sayings in rhyme form:

Worship no other gods but Me,
Before no idol bend your knee.
Take not the name of God in vain,
Nor dare the Sabbath day profane.
Give both your parents honour due,
Take heed that you no murder do.
Abstain from words and deeds unclean,
Nor steal though you be poor and mean
Nor make a wilful lie and love it,
What is your neighbour's do not covet.

Although women are not required to observe as many commandments as men, Jewish tradition teaches that women were asked before men whether they wished to accept the Torah. The reason given was because women are more prompt in the fulfilment of the commandments. Another reason was that women would be more eager to introduce their children to the study of the Torah.

The Torah is not limited to one faith or one people. According to tradition, when God gave the Torah His voice split up into 70 voices in 70 languages so that all nations could understand. Non-Jews, however, are not under an obligation to keep all 613 commandments. They need to keep only seven, known as the Seven Laws of Noah, or **Noachide Laws**. Non-Jews who keep these seven laws are considered as if they had kept the entire 613. These seven are timeless and not bound by when and where you live. They

can help to keep our world civilized, and make it a better and more peaceful place. The Seven Laws of Noah are:

1 Do not worship idols
2 Do not blaspheme
3 Do not murder
4 Do not steal
5 Do not commit immoral acts
6 Do not be cruel to animals
7 Set up and maintain courts of justice

There is also the following statement from the Talmud, which shows that the Torah is universal and for everyone:

'The Torah was given in the third month, the zodiac symbol of which is Gemini, to show that it was for both Jacob (Jew) and Esau (non-Jew) [the famous twins mentioned in the first book of the Torah].'

NEW WORD

Noachide Laws seven laws named after Noah, which should be kept by all non-Jewish people

THINGS TO DO

1 Write the Seven Laws of Noah in your note books and add a sentence or two explaining each of these.

2 Discuss whether the world would be a better place if everyone tried to keep the Noachide Laws. Are there any other laws you would want to add to the list?

3 **a** Compare the Ten Commandments and the Seven Laws of Noah.

b Write down the three laws missing from the Seven Laws of Noah. What value might they have for non-Jews?

A yad, or pointer, used when reading the Torah.

This section deals with some facts and customs with regard to the Torah.

- Selling a Torah scroll is considered a sign of disrespect.
- A Torah scroll has the highest degree of holiness. No other object, even a printed Tanach or prayerbook, may be placed on it.
- About 1,900 years ago, some leading rabbis permitted Torah scrolls to be written in Greek, but not in any other language.
- It is customary to fast if a Torah scroll is dropped.
- The longest verse in the Tanach is *Esther* 8:9, which contains 43 words.
- The dog is mentioned in the Tanach eighteen times, but the cat is not mentioned even once.
- Breast-stroke is mentioned in *Isaiah* 25:11: 'as a swimmer spreads out his hands to swim'.
- The last sentence of the Torah scroll is always written in the middle of the line, to show that one can never really complete the Torah, which is endless.
- Why does each **tractate** of the Talmud begin with page two and not page one? To remind us that no matter how much we study and learn, we have not yet come to the first page!
- Some Orthodox Jews sway the body when studying the Torah or praying. This takes place in both sitting and standing positions. The reason is that the whole body should be working together in study or prayer.

The following words of wisdom come from the Talmud:

> 'He who has compassion upon his fellows may be considered a true descendant of Abraham.'

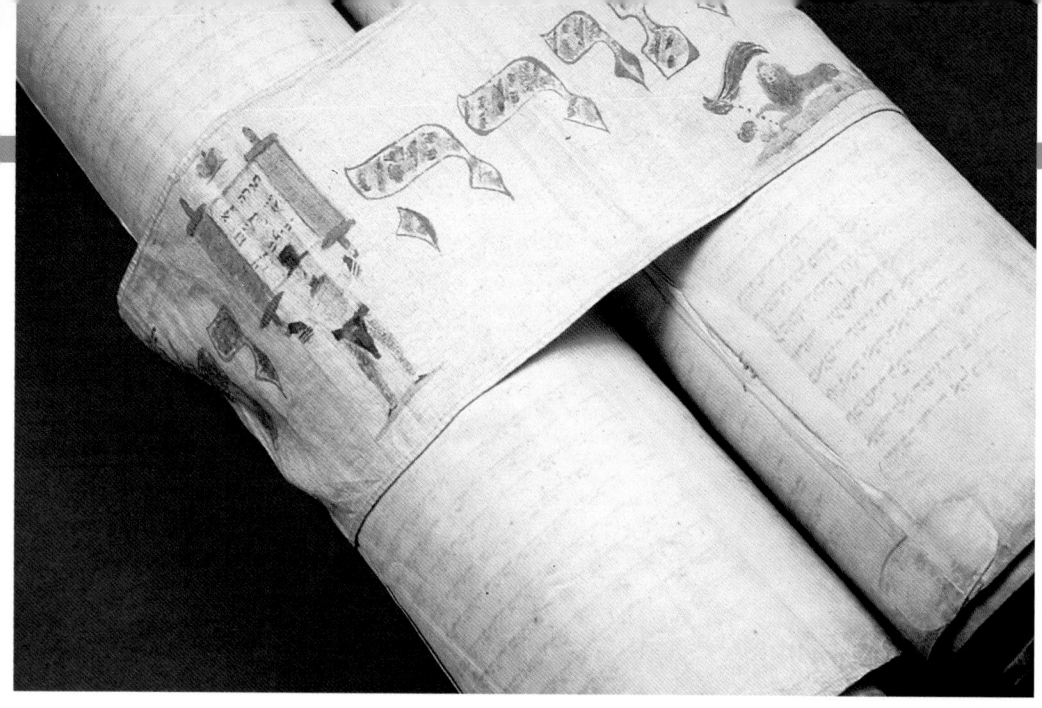

A decorated Torah binder.

'Let a person first lead the good life, then ask God for religious truth.'

'Why was man created a solitary human being, without a companion? So that it might not be said that some races are superior to others.'

'Who is the bravest hero? He who turns an enemy into a friend.'

'When a person appears before the Throne of Judgement, the first question asked is not "Have you believed in God?" or "Have you prayed or performed ritual acts?" but "Have you dealt honourably in all your dealings with your fellow?".'

'An evil tongue hurts three people: the one who speaks, the one who listens, and the one who is talked about.'

'The world exists for the sake of three things: the study of Torah, the worship of God, and acts of loving kindness.'

'Do not limit a child to your own learning, for he was born in another time.'

'To learn Torah it is best to go to one teacher. To discuss it it is better to go to several teachers. The many different explanations will help to give you understanding.'

'Why are the words of Torah like fire? A fire is built by many logs and the words of Torah survive only through many minds.'

After studying the Torah one concludes with a prayer of the rabbis, part of which reads:

'Unto Israel and unto the rabbis, and unto their pupils and the pupils of their pupils, and unto all who engage in the study of Torah, in this or any other place, unto them and unto you be great peace and favour, love, mercy, a life of fulfilment and of plenty, and salvation from their Heavenly Father. Amen.'

NEW WORD

Tractate a volume of the Talmud covering a specific subject such as marriage

THINGS TO DO

1 How do Jews show respect for the Torah?

2 Explain why many people think that it is important to treat religious books with special respect.

3 Write down the three sentences that you like most. Discuss your list with someone else.

Glossary

Bar Mitzvah a 'son of the commandment'; a thirteen-year-old boy who is accepted as a religious adult

Bat Mitzvah a 'daughter of the commandment'; a twelve-year-old girl who is accepted as a religious adult

Bedouin an Arab of the desert, who often wanders around

Cheder classes for Jewish children, held in rooms attached to a synagogue, where they learn Jewish subjects

Circumcision cutting off the foreskin; a ritual which is practised on all Jewish baby boys

Desecrate break or disobey a sacred occasion, place or ritual

Essenes a Jewish group which helped to write and preserve the Dead Sea Scrolls

Ethics how we should behave

Greggors hand-held rattles which make a loud, rasping noise when waved round

Holocaust the murder of six million Jews by the Nazis during the Second World War

Ketuvim a Hebrew word meaning 'writings'. It includes the later books of the Tanach and books like *Psalms*

Kosher a Hebrew word meaning 'fit'. According to the Torah, Jews can only eat kosher animals, that is animals that have split hooves and chew the cud, such as the ox or goat, but not the pig or rabbit. For a full list of kosher animals, fish and birds, see chapter 11 of the book of *Leviticus*

Messiah a human being chosen by God to usher in peace for the Jewish people and all the world

Mezuzah (plural mezuzot) a parchment scroll which is placed in a small case and fixed to the doorposts of Jewish homes

Midrash (plural midrashim) a collection of writings, many in the form of stories, which make up the Oral Torah; or one of this collection

Minyan a quorum – the minimum number of people needed – to make a Jewish meeting valid

Nevi'im the books of the prophets

Noachide Laws seven laws named after Noah, which should be kept by all non-Jewish people

Parables stories which teach a moral lesson

Pesach (Passover) the week-long spring festival which celebrates the freedom from Egyptian slavery

Rabbi the spiritual leader of a synagogue who conducts services, teaches adults and children, and has other duties similar to a Minister in other religions

Rosh Hashanah the Jewish New Year, which is celebrated in September or October

Shabbat the Jewish day of rest. This is the seventh day of the week, Saturday, as mentioned in the Ten Commandments

Shema one of the most important Jewish prayers, recited every morning and evening

Sofer a Jewish scribe who writes Torah scrolls and mezuzot (plural for mezuzah) by hand

Synagogue a Greek word for a Jewish house of worship. In Hebrew it is known as Beth ha Knesset. It is also often called shul, from the German word for school

Tallit a four-cornered prayer shawl worn by male worshippers at morning services. In some Progressive synagogues, women also wear them

Talmud the collection of writings which make up the Oral Torah

Tanach a word made from the letters T (Torah), N (Nevi'im) and K, pronounced 'ch' (Ketuvim), meaning the Hebrew Bible

Temple the central Jewish place of worship in Jerusalem. Both the First and Second Temples were destroyed and none has existed for 2,000 years, as they were replaced by synagogues

Tephilin the two small leather boxes and straps worn at weekday morning services

Torah teaching or instruction: the first five books of the Bible

Tractate a volume of the Talmud covering a specific subject such as marriage

Violate break a law or agreement

Yeshiva a college usually for men, where they study the Talmud in depth

Yom Kippur a fast day which takes place nine days after Rosh Hashanah